*Stamps Tell
the Story of
John F. Kennedy*

Books by Emery Kelen

Peace Is an Adventure
Stamps Tell the Story of the United Nations
Stamps Tell the Story of John F. Kennedy

Stamps Tell the Story of John F. Kennedy

by emery kelen

MEREDITH PRESS NEW YORK

Library of Congress Catalog Card
Number: 68–28724
Manufactured in the United States
of America for Meredith Press

I am greatly indebted to
J. & H. STOLOW, INC.
Stamp dealers
New York, New York
for having provided me
with the stamps used
in this book

THE MAN AND THE LEGEND

A President of the United States is the head of state and commander in chief of the Army, Navy, and Air Force. And he is something more: As the elected leader of a nation, he has the special relationship to the people of having been chosen by them to represent them, to be a national image. Whether we have elected a father image, a son image, an ideal image, or a favorite-uncle image is something the popular psychologists decide about each President.

One thing is certain: We leave our Presidents little private life. The White House is a glass house with all of us looking in, and since the advent of television the image has become all the keener, clearer, and closer.

The Kennedy image is especially close to all Americans. We remember him vividly as a handsome young man, rather too young looking to be President, neatly dressed, but always seeming informal, even careless, because he rarely wore an overcoat, and his thick hair couldn't bear a hat. We saw that he was a playful father of an attractive family. We listened and watched when he made speeches, and at his press conferences noted the swift, metallic "Harvard" voice and the hand jabbing the air downward as he emphasized his points. We were eyewitnesses on the cold January day when, bareheaded and without overcoat, he made his inaugural address. That was the day we became aware that there was something behind this image—a man of rare strength and rare idealism.

We visited the White House when the First Lady was hostess and showed us around her newly decorated rooms. With her we entered the presidential office, saw the President and how his eyes lighted when his small son emerged from under the desk where affairs of state were transacted. We stood at his grave, and we watched when John Junior gave a last salute to the coffin. We shared the grief of his widow, and like his real family, we felt ourselves bereft.

Then, ennobled by the immense sorrow of a nation and dimmed by time, the popular image became a cherished memory. A Kennedy legend was in the making. One day, like the Lincoln legend, it might obscure the man.

But President Kennedy was a man who should not be forgotten; nor should his actions and words, his strength and idealism, be obscured by legend. They should be remembered and used for future action. He was the man who signed the first nuclear test ban treaty to save succeeding generations from atomic radiation. He founded the Peace Corps and filled young Americans with his own determination to help young nations help themselves. He brought to life the Alliance for Progress to assist our neighbors in Latin America. He asked Congress for the strongest civil rights bill passed in a hundred years. He stood for disarmament, for reconciliation between East and West, and he stood for peace.

He placed before the nation a new challenge and new horizons. He was a doer and a dreamer. He did what he had to do and dreamed what he would have preferred to have done. He left us his dreams, and they are our best hope for a tomorrow.

Four days after his tragic death, the United Nations General Assembly held a Commemorative Meeting. Secretary-General U Thant said, " . . . the loss is not only a loss to his bereaved family whose head he was, nor even the country over whose destiny he presided with rare ability and distinction as Head of State. It is a loss suffered by the entire world, by all humanity, for the late President embodied a rare and quite remarkable combination of intellect and courage, of vigor and compassion, of devotion to the arts and sciences, which was focused on serving his basic concern for the well-being of all mankind."

The following pages present stamps published in commemoration of this vital young American President, issued in his honor by countries large and small all over the world.

YOUTH

John Fitzgerald Kennedy was born May 29, 1917, in Brookline, Massachusetts, of an Irish-American family. His forefathers had come to these shores from Ireland in the great wave of immigration that followed the potato famine in 1846–47. In time, John's great-grandfather Kennedy established himself as a cooper, a dealer in barrels such as the kind used for beer. It is not surprising that his son, Patrick J. Kennedy, John's grandfather, became a saloon-keeper, but he soon drifted into Boston politics where he made the acquaintance of that colorful Mayor of Boston, three-times Congressman, and Massachusetts State Senator, John F. Fitzgerald or "Honey Fitz."

In due course Patrick's son, young Joseph P. Kennedy, married John F. Fitzgerald's daughter, Rose, and they had nine children, of whom John Fitzgerald was the second son. Joseph became a successful businessman, and eventually, under President Franklin Delano Roosevelt, he entered the diplomatic service and became Ambassador to the Court of St. James. The young Kennedys grew up in a cosmopolitan household.

They were a close-knit family, intensely loyal to each other and presenting a united front to the outside world. But among themselves they competed fiercely. Both boys and girls could play a thumping game of touch football, and one or another of them usually had a bandage on. Sometimes they would knock each other unconscious.

This stamp, issued by the Kingdom of Yemen shows the President when he was nine years old, in 1926.

Yemen, about the size of Nebraska, is an ancient mountainous land, bordering the Red Sea, near the southern tip of the Arabian peninsula. It has a population of about five million. Mocha coffee, dates, herbs, fruits, charcoal, and precious stones are its main exports.

Colors: black, gold, cherry red

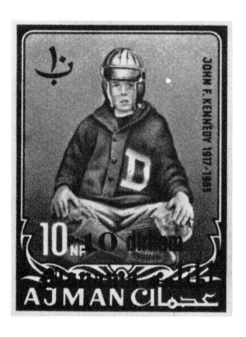

Jack, as the future President was familiarly called, went to the Dexter School in Brookline, Massachusetts, where he was a member of the football team. He was not the huskiest of the Kennedys, but he made up for a rather fragile build by enthusiasm and tremendous drive. When he was nine years old his father settled one million dollars on him, as he did upon all his children. In the fall of 1931, he was sent to the Choate School at Wallingford, Connecticut, a skinny boy with a face full of freckles. One of his report cards is preserved for us, but there is no suggestion here of a future President. It noted that his room was disorderly, being used, as a rule, as a club for his friends. "Jack studies at the last minute, keeps appointments late, has little sense of material value and can seldom locate his possessions." And yet the headmaster of Choate School glanced into the future when he wrote to Jack's father: "Jack has a clever, individualistic mind . . . his natural gift of an individual outlook and witty expression are going to help him. . . . We must allow for a period of adjustment and growing up; and the final product is often more interesting and more effective than the boy with a more conventional mind who has been to us, parents and teachers, much less trouble."

Well said, headmaster! The lives of great men quite often remind us that their boyhoods are far from sublime.

Colors: black, green, cherry red

HARVARD YEARS

Before entering college, Jack was sent for the summer to the London School of Economics where he rubbed elbows with Europeans, Indians, Australians, Africans, all of whom had come to study under the noted socialist professor, Harold J. Laski.

In the fall of 1936 he entered Harvard, where his father and elder brother, Joseph Junior, had gone before him. He studied law, but he found time to practice swimming, which saved his life in World War II, as we shall see.

One of his tutors, the well-known economist Kenneth Galbraith, described him in his Harvard days as "gay and charming, irreverent, good-looking, and far from diligent." Yet in 1940 he graduated *cum laude* in political science. When he became President he sent his former tutor, Galbraith, as his Ambassador to India. "A period of penance," he told him with a smile.

8

This stamp was issued by Ajman, one of the seven states of Trucial Oman, situated on the peninsula that separates the Persian Gulf and the Gulf of Oman. The term "trucial" refers to the treaty that seven sheiks of this region signed with Britain early in the nineteenth century. Previously the sheiks had waged war against British shipping in the Gulf, not only in order to preserve their independence, but because piracy was a traditional occupation in these waters. After the truce, however, they abjured sea warfare in return for Britain's promise to guarantee their independence. The peoples of the Trucial States are said to be of "pure" Arab stock. Certainly, they have preserved the Arab way of life almost unchanged since ancient times.

Colors: black, blue, pink

WAR HERO

In 1939, while playing football, Jack suffered an injury to his back which was to plague him for the rest of his life. In that year Hitler was preparing to make war. Jack, a junior at Harvard, spent six months in England working for his father, who was Ambassador. At the same time he wrote his college thesis, choosing as his theme a history of the events that led to World War II. Later, this thesis was published in book form under the title *Why England Slept,* and it became a national best seller.

In the spring of 1941, Kennedy tried to enlist in the army, but he was rejected because of his back injury. He performed strengthening exercises and managed to pass a Navy fitness test in the fall. He was stationed in Washington, but on December 7, 1941, the day of Pearl Harbor, he applied for sea duty. His father used his influence to get him into a Motor Torpedo Boat Squadron. In March, 1943, he was flown to the Solomon Islands and given command of PT-109.

One starless night, Lieutenant Kennedy's PT-109 was patrolling Blackett Strait in mid-Solomons when out of the

darkness a Japanese destroyer appeared and cut the boat in two. The survivors managed to stay afloat through the night wearing life preservers. When day broke they desperately hoped that they would be rescued by another PT boat patrolling in the area, but none came. "We'll swim to that island," said Kennedy. One of his men was badly wounded. Kennedy cut loose one end of a long strap from the man's life preserver and took the end in his teeth. He swam breast stroke, pulling the helpless man on his back.

It took over five hours to reach the barren island. After exploration had disclosed no fresh water, Kennedy decided that the group would swim to a larger island. Again he took his wounded shipmate's strap between his teeth and swam for three hours. On the larger island they found coconuts lying on the ground, and, breaking them open, gratefully drank the milk.

On the fourth day, Lieutenant Kennedy and one of his shipmates swam to an island called Nauru. There some natives found them, and Kennedy, picking up a coconut with a smooth shell, scratched a message on it with a jackknife: "Eleven alive, native knows posit and reefs Nauru Island, Kennedy." He gave it to the islanders, hoping they would know what to do with it.

On the sixth day, in the morning, four husky natives appeared. One walked up to Kennedy and said in perfect English, "I have a letter for you, sir." It was an answer from the commander of a New Zealand patrol, operating from another part of the island.

The natives packed Kennedy in the bottom of their canoe and paddled with him to the New Zealanders' headquarters. The officer came to the water's edge and said with stiff formality, "How do you do. Leftenant Wincote."

"Hello," said Jack. "I'm Kennedy."

"Well, come up to my tent and have a cup of tea."

John Kennedy was awarded the purple heart and the Navy and Marine Corps Medal for his "extremely heroic conduct," which had been "unmindful of personal danger." As for the coconut shell on which he had scratched his message, it was kept encased in plastic on the President's desk in the White House as long as he lived. Once a schoolboy asked him how he had come to be a war hero. Kennedy replied, "It was easy—they sank my boat."

Colors: black, gold, pink
green, gold, pink
blue, sepia

THE POLITICIAN

By December, 1943, Lt. Jack Kennedy was sent back to the United States. He had come down with malaria, and the old back injury had continued to trouble him. The following year there came bad news. His elder brother, Joseph Kennedy, Jr., had been killed in action. He had volunteered for an experimental mission—flying a Liberator bomber, loaded with explosives, from which he was to have bailed out after a control plane had directed it upon its target in Germany. But while the plane was still over England it disintegrated with a tremendous blast.

Jack had deeply admired his elder brother, who had been a handsome and gifted young man, sociable and gay. In fact, Joseph had been the son slated to continue the family political traditions. Jack had thought of becoming a lawyer, a journalist, or perhaps a history professor; or he might enter the Foreign Service. But now he stepped into his brother's shoes. In 1946, aged twenty-nine, he announced his candidacy for congressman in the Eleventh District in Massachusetts.

He was elected and served three terms.

In 1952, the year Dwight D. Eisenhower was elected President, Kennedy defeated Henry Cabot Lodge, the promoter of Eisenhower's presidency, to become Senator from Massachusetts.

This stamp was issued by Fujeira, situated on the east coast of the Gulf of Oman, and one of the seven states of Trucial Oman ruled by Arab sheiks.

Colors: black, gold, light pink

MARRIAGE

In the spring of 1951, John F. Kennedy attended a dinner party and there met Jacqueline Bouvier. "I leaned across the asparagus," he said later, "and asked her for a date." Jacqueline denied this story; she said asparagus had not been on the menu.

"It was a very spasmodic courtship," Mrs. Kennedy tells us. "We did not see each other for six months." When she went on a visit to Europe, he campaigned in Massachusetts. While she lived in Washington, Jack spent half of each year in Massachusetts. "He'd call me from some oyster bar," she said, "with a great clanking of coins, to ask me out to the movies the following Wednesday in Washington. He loved Westerns and Civil War pictures. He was not the candy-and-flowers type, so every now and then he'd give me a book."

After a courtship of two and a half years, they were married in St. Mary's Roman Catholic Church in Newport,

Rhode Island. It was September 12, 1953, and the Most Reverend Richard J. Cushing, Archbishop of Boston, performed the ceremony.

Jacqueline Bouvier's ancestors had come over from France to fight under the flag of Lafayette for the liberty of America. Some had returned to France, and others had stayed. Jacqueline had gone to Vassar and to the Sorbonne in Paris, and she spoke fluent French, as well as Italian, Spanish, and even a little Polish.

Colors: royal blue, gold, sepia

THE ROCKING CHAIR

Kennedy's health was not good during these early years as a politician and young husband. His back injury had gotten worse. He often needed crutches to move around.

The first year of his marriage he decided that he would rather undergo an extremely dangerous spinal operation than carry on with crutches. The aftereffects of the surgery were almost fatal to him. Twice he was given up, his family summoned to his bedside, and he was given the last rites of the Church. But he fought back and recovered. The following February, 1955, he was obliged to go back on the operating table to endure still another almost fatal operation, as a metal plate placed in his spine in the earlier surgery was removed.

It was while he was convalescing in Palm Beach that he wrote his Pulitzer Prize–winning book, *Profiles in Courage,* telling of men in American history who had stood up for their convictions against criticism and ruin.

In May, 1955, after an absence of almost a year, he returned to Washington. But until the end of his life he always wore a cloth brace and corrective shoes, and he slept with a bed board under his mattress. When he traveled, staying at hotels where no bed board was available, his mattress was moved to the floor. To ease his pain, he kept a rocking chair in his office in Washington; and this chair became a trademark of his presidency.

Yemen, which issued this stamp, was once part of the ancient kingdom of Sheba. The Bible speaks of its gold, spices, and precious stones as gifts borne by the Queen of Sheba to King Solomon.

Colors: orange, gold, brown

CAROLINE

On November 27, 1957, at New York Hospital, a daughter was born to the Kennedys—Caroline. Lovers of statistics will be pleased to know that she weighed seven pounds, two ounces. Seventeen days later, she was christened by the former Archbishop Richard Cushing, now Cardinal Cushing, at St. Patrick's Cathedral in New York. Her godfather was Senator Robert F. Kennedy.

As she grew older, Caroline became the owner of a private zoo consisting of two ducks presented by her father; two hamsters, Debbie and Billie, who one day would make themselves famous by breaking out of their cage and hiding under the presidential bed; Robin the canary; Macaroni the pony; and a number of cats and dogs.

Caroline was far from an oppressed minority in the senatorial household. She was a full-fledged member of the family, who, when her parents were reading or working, was not deported to the nursery, but sat with them, reading a state paper entitled *Peter Rabbit*. When her mother painted, Caroline sat on the floor next to her, playing with crayons or using her own paint set.

Colors: black, green, sepia

HYANNIS PORT

Kennedy's usual greeting for his daughter was "Hiya, Buttons!" He was a loving father, not only as a display for the photographers, but in a subdued, smiling, constant way.

After the tussle of politics he liked to return to Hyannis Port for the weekends to enjoy the sea, the sun, and family life. He would collect Caroline and his many nieces and nephews in a jeep and drive them to the nearest candy store for a treat. For them he was never a Senator, or even the President. He was plain Jack, or else "Uncle Jack."

Skippering his family and the numerous Kennedy brood on his boat was his favorite recreation. Swimming was one of the few sports his back permitted him to enjoy.

His favorite food was a bowl of steaming fish chowder, especially after a cold swim.

Colors: black, gold, light green   **20**

POSTAGE بوريد

FUJEIRA الفجيرة

JOHN F KENNEDY 1917·1963

Caroline was no problem child. She was full of fun and made friends easily. The day was close at hand when she would become one of the most famous and popular little girls in the world. In fact, a Republican once said of her, "She is the Democrats' one secret weapon we can't fight."

In spite of her busy life, Mrs. Kennedy found time to spend with Caroline and to provide for her a family life with her parents. "I am not much of a cook," said Jacqueline. "I love to read and love to paint, and I love my baby. I don't want my children to be raised by nurses and secret servicemen."

And so, in Georgetown on Halloween, Jacqueline Kennedy went for a trick-or-treat expedition with Caroline.

"No matter what else I might achieve, if my children turned out badly, I should feel that I had failed," she said once. And she added, "I'm sure my husband would, too."

Colors: black, gold   **21**

ON THE CAMPAIGN TRAIL

On January 2, 1960, at a press conference in Washington, D. C., John Fitzgerald Kennedy said, "I am announcing today my candidacy for the presidency of the United States." On July 13, 1960, in Los Angeles, he received the nomination for the presidency on the first ballot. He chose as his running mate Senator Lyndon B. Johnson from Texas, who had competed with him for the nomination.

A strenuous campaign followed in which the entire Kennedy family—mother, sisters, brothers, brothers-in-law—took active part. (Joseph Kennedy was unable to participate because of illness.) As his campaign manager, Jack chose his brother Robert, the late Senator from New York. From state to state, from door to door, he campaigned. During 1960 alone, he traveled some 65,000 air miles in more than two dozen states and he made some 350 speeches. "He doesn't eat, he doesn't sleep, he doesn't do anything to keep fit," observed his wife, "but he thrives on it."

He held debates on television with the Republican candidate, Vice-President Richard M. Nixon. It was estimated that seventy million adults, nearly two-thirds of the nation, watched the first debate, the largest campaign audience ever. His intelligence, charm, and quick wit lighted the screen. The debates were thought to have contributed greatly to his ultimate victory.

The state that issued this stamp, Ras al Khaima, is another of the seven sheikdoms of Trucial Oman. Fishing and pearling are the main industries. The state's coastal plain is rather arid, and Tomb Island, in the entrance of the Gulf, is noted for its poisonous snakes.

Colors: black, blue, ocher

Three factors militated against the election of John F. Kennedy for President: his youth, his lack of experience, and his Catholic religion. Since the United States is predominantly a Protestant country, it has always elected Protestant Presidents.

His youth was soon seen to be an asset. As the first presidential candidate born in the twentieth century, he appealed to young voters who felt that "he is one of us." His Catholicism, however, was a hotly debated issue. "I am not the Catholic candidate for President," he kept assuring the nation. "I am the Democratic Party's candidate, who happens to be a Catholic." In an address to the American Society of Newspaper Editors, he said, "Are we to say that a Jew can be elected Mayor of Dublin, a Protestant can be named Foreign Minister of France, a Moslem can sit in the Israeli Parliament, but a Catholic cannot be President of the United States?"

In his opinion, the Church he believed in was important

24

to him alone. What mattered was the kind of America he believed in.

This stamp, issued in Costa Rica, shows John F. Kennedy praying in the Cathedral of San José, the capital, during his visit to that country. Costa Rica, the southernmost state of Central America, is slightly smaller than West Virginia, and has a population of 1.5 million. The principal exports are coffee, bananas, cocoa, cattle, cotton, fish, and abaca.

Colors: black, blue, orange

By no means all the Democratic leaders of those days supported the candidacy of John F. Kennedy. Mrs. Eleanor Roosevelt, with whom Kennedy is pictured on this stamp, had supported the candidacy of Adlai Stevenson at the Democratic Convention. She thought Kennedy was inexperienced, and she said that she hoped his "unselfishness and courage" would induce him to take the vice-presidency, where he would have "the opportunity to grow and learn."

Former President Truman in a nationally televised interview asked bluntly, "Senator, are you certain that you are quite ready for the country or that the country is ready for you in the role of President?" Truman also thought that we needed "a man with the greatest possible maturity and experience," and he urged Kennedy to be patient.

In a televised press conference, Kennedy answered Truman. "If all those below the age of forty-four had been ex-

26

cluded from positions of trust and command," he said, "that would have kept Jefferson from writing the Declaration of Independence, Washington from commanding the Continental Army, Madison from fathering the Constitution . . . and Christopher Columbus from even discovering America."

On November 8, 1960, by a slim majority of two hundred thousand, he was elected thirty-fifth President of the United States.

Colors: cherry red, olive green

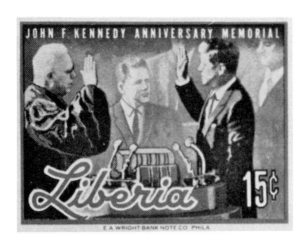

INAUGURATION

January 20, 1961, the day of the inauguration was clear but bitter cold. The day before, a blizzard had blanketed the city with eight inches of snow, and during the night seven hundred plows and trucks had performed the task of digging Washington, D. C., out of it.

The President-elect had taken a lively interest in the planning of the inauguration ceremony. He asked Robert Frost to read a poem and Marian Anderson to sing the "Star-Spangled Banner." He provided the Kennedy family Bible on which to take the oath of office. He indicated that top hats would be worn by the official party.

When Cardinal Cushing delivered a prayer for the new President, a short circuit made the lectern smolder. Secret servicemen and firemen busied themselves to put out the fire. The new President repeated the oath of office after Chief Justice Earl Warren, and in a clear voice echoed, "So help me God!"

Then after he had delivered his inaugural address, in the twenty-degree cold, he watched the inaugural parade. It took four hours to march by. In the evening he attended the five inaugural balls, held simultaneously in various hotels. He was handsome, smiling Jack, the pride of the Irish and the hope of the country. His very attractive and elegant wife with the enormous warmth of her smile and a manner of shy graciousness was at his side. No one could have guessed on inauguration day that exactly a thousand days later he would be buried by Cardinal Cushing and that Chief Justice Warren would head the commission that investigated his death.

Liberia, the country that issued this stamp, is an independent African republic, slightly larger than the state of Ohio. It has valuable mineral resources.

Colors: black, red

"Ask not what your country can do for you—ask what you can do for your country." This is the most famous quotation from the Kennedy inaugural address, which the principality of Monaco, on the Mediterranean Sea, chose to place on this commemorative stamp—mistakenly using the word "will" instead of "can."

The President took great care in the preparation of his first address to the people. He had asked his special assistant, Theodore C. Sorensen, to read all past inaugural addresses, and asked him to study Lincoln's Gettysburg Address and find out why it has been so long remembered. From Billy Graham, the evangelist, he obtained a list of possible Bible quotations, and a similar list was asked of Isaac Franck, the Director of Washington's Jewish Community Council.

Kennedy's inaugural address was one of the best speeches any of us will ever hear. It was delivered in difficult circumstances. He stood in the cold, surrounded by people huddled against the wind, but the dry air carried his words clear cut as an icicle across the crowd. "Let every nation know, whether it wishes us well or ill, that we shall pay any price, bear any burden, meet any hardship, support any friend, oppose any foe to assure the survival and the success of liberty."

The affairs of the nation, indeed the affairs of much of the world, had for years been paralyzed by the cold war which prevented communication between East and West. People everywhere waited to hear what the new President would say about it, and his words, when they came, pointed to new directions: "Let us never negotiate out of fear. But let us never fear to negotiate."

To the nation's adversaries he said, "Let both sides explore what problems unite us instead of belaboring those problems that divide us. . . . let both sides join in creating a new endeavor, not a new balance of power, but a new world of law, where the strong are just and the weak secure and the peace preserved. . . .

"But let us begin," said John F. Kennedy.

Monaco, which issued this stamp, is a small principality on the Mediterranean. It is noted for its exceptionally mild climate and magnificent scenery; its main industry is tourism.

Colors: black, blue

Among the first to congratulate Kennedy was the outgoing President Dwight D. Eisenhower. At the inaugural ceremonies the former President, who was seventy, sat, bald-headed, stoical as a soldier against the cold, listening attentively to the young Kennedy with his enviable warm cap of thick hair. The contrast in age seemed to be a fitting illustration to the sentence in the inaugural address: "Let the word go forth from this time and place, to friend and foe alike, that the torch has been passed to a new generation of Americans."

He was not indifferent to the emotions Eisenhower must have felt on that day. In New York, he had jokingly asked the former President of the United Nations General Assembly, Frederick H. Boland of Ireland, how it felt to be an ex-President. More seriously he asked the same question of Truman on the evening of inauguration day, and he reflected on what adjustment Dwight Eisenhower might have made—waking up in the morning as President and the same afternoon going home as a private citizen.

Colors: black, gold, light green

POSTAGE

FUJEIRA

JOHN F. KENNEDY 1917-1963

VISITING EUROPE

In the summer of 1961, the new President, accompanied by Mrs. Kennedy, traveled to Europe to meet face to face the leaders with whom he would have to deal. The first stop was in Paris to see President Charles de Gaulle. Thereafter he was to meet Nikita Khrushchev in Vienna, and finally talk with British Prime Minister Harold Macmillan in London.

In the splendid Palace of Versailles, built for Louis XIV, the "Sun King," the President and his wife were accorded a reception as brilliant as any they could have imagined. In the Hall of Mirrors a hundred and fifty guests dined by candlelight, using the gold-trimmed china that the City of Paris had given to Napoleon as a coronation gift.

Fashionable Jacqueline Kennedy was a dazzling success in

Paris. Her charm, femininity, and especially her mastery of French, turned out to be political assets in the French capital. Jokingly, yet with visible pride, the President told a Parisian audience: "I do not feel it inappropriate for me to introduce myself. I am the man who accompanied Jacqueline Kennedy to Paris."

The stamp shows him, with Mrs. Kennedy, talking to André Malraux, Minister of Cultural Affairs and a famous French author.

Colors: black, gold, light pink

In Vienna, both the Americans and the Russians were received magnificently in the former imperial palaces of the Hapsburgs, and the city displayed all its old-world gaiety and charm.

But Kennedy had grave matters to discuss with Premier Khrushchev: disarmament, the nuclear test ban, and, above all, the dangerous situation that had developed in Berlin.

After World War II, a four-power administration had been set up in Berlin, but the city was situated one hundred miles within the East German territory, which was controlled by Soviet troops. The city itself was split into communist East Berlin and non-communist West Berlin. Later, the two segments of the city were further separated by the famous Berlin Wall.

In Vienna, Khrushchev was threatening to sign a separate peace treaty with communist East Germany. This would have ended the four-power administration of Berlin, for access to the city would have fallen entirely under communist

35

control. The President felt that he could not permit this. He said firmly that if our access to Berlin was cut off, the United States would fight. Khrushchev told him that he would meet force with force. They could not agree.

Kennedy told the Russian premier, "Mr. Chairman, it's going to be a cold winter." These were his last words to Khrushchev in Vienna.

Khrushchev did not sign a separate treaty with East Germany.

Wherever the President went on his travels, he was followed by a team of army officers, one of whom carried a slender black case. This contained the secret codes with which, by presidential order, a signal could be given for nuclear retaliation.

This stamp, issued by the West German government is to honor the memory of a friend. The Federal Republic of Germany is about the size of Oregon and has a population of almost sixty million. It is a highly industrialized country, one of the parties to the North Atlantic Treaty Organization.

Color: blue

ENTER JOHN JUNIOR

John Fitzgerald Kennedy, Jr., was born on November 25, 1960, just two months before his father's inauguration. By the end of his first year in the White House he was beginning to make himself at home in the world.

Everything that flew intrigued him: planes, rockets, blimps, and his father's helicopter, which he pronounced "heprecops." His favorite place to play was under his father's desk, which had a little secret door that could be closed when he wished to hide. He called the place "my house."

It was great fun, too, to climb on the conference table or to ride on the presidential rocking chair.

Caroline and John Junior were unusually bright, inquisitive children with a sufficient amount of surplus energy, and they were as prone to mischief in the White House as any children in any house. One day Caroline appeared at a press conference wearing her mother's shoes. And once she wandered into the press lobby to report that her father was "sitting upstairs with his shoes and socks off not doing anything."

She asked Speaker Sam Rayburn why he didn't have any hair.

Like most American mothers, Jacqueline read the book of the famous baby doctor, Benjamin Spock, and found it a relief to know that other people's children were "just as bad" at the same age.

Colors: black, light green, sepia

THE BOOKISH PRESIDENT

Kennedy became known as a bookish President. His reading had a wide range: newspapers, Irish poets, American history, Greek classics, Shakespeare, Robert Frost. Once in a single speech he quoted from Wilson, Goethe, Faulkner, Swift, Emerson, Asquith, and Tennyson. He memorized poems and taught Caroline to do so, too.

While he was still a Senator, he and his brother Bobby had enrolled in Baltimore in a speed-reading course, and he could read twelve hundred words a minute. He had an unusual ability, also, to remember accurately what he read.

He read books, and he wrote books. *Why England Slept* had been a best seller. *Profiles in Courage* got the Pulitzer Prize. He edited a private volume about his brother, *As We Remember Joe.* His collected speeches made up two volumes, *The Strategy of Peace* and *To Turn the Tide.*

During his administration, learning and culture were openly in vogue at the White House, and this served to make Americans everywhere conscious of the value of an excellent educational system. "The quality of American life," said the President, "must keep pace with the quantity of American goods. This country cannot afford to be materially rich and spiritually poor."

The kingdom of Burundi, a country the size of Maryland in east Central Africa, was part of the Belgian U.N. trusteeship territory of Ruanda-Urundi. It became independent on July 1, 1962. Its main crop is coffee, which is the principal export.

Colors: green, light pink

REPUBLIQUE DU TCHAD
100F
POSTE AERIENNE
President John F. KENNEDY
1917-1963
Discours sur les droits civiques - 11 Juin 1963
H AUBRY   DELRIEU

CIVIL RIGHTS

The Republic of Chad, a former French colony in equatorial Africa, chose to commemorate on this stamp Kennedy's speech on civil rights, delivered on June 11, 1963, and broadcast over radio and television.

He said, "One hundred years of delay have passed since President Lincoln freed the slaves, yet their heirs, their grandsons, are not fully free. They are not yet freed from the bonds of injustice. They are not yet freed from social and economic oppression, and this nation, for all its hopes and all its boasts, will not be fully free until all its citizens are free. . . .

"We preach freedom around the world, and we mean it, and we cherish our freedom here at home; but are we to say to the world and, much more importantly, to each other that this is a land of the free except for the Negroes; that we have no second-class citizens except Negroes; that we

41

have no class or caste system, no ghettos, no master race, except with respect to Negroes?"

In the summer of 1963, President Kennedy sponsored the most far-reaching legislation in the field of civil rights that had ever been proposed by any President. It was passed in the House of Representatives, and then in 1964 passed in the Senate in the form President Kennedy had suggested.

Kennedy delivered his speech on civil rights from the White House, seated at his desk. The postal authorities of Chad took the artistic liberty of representing him standing. It made a better picture.

Chad, a country about four-fifths the size of Alaska, became independent in 1960. It has a population of approximately 3.5 million.

Colors: brown, blue, pink

AFRICA

It is most appropriate that the independent Negro Republic of Liberia, founded in 1822 by freed Negroes from the United States, should commemorate the death of President Kennedy, a champion of civil rights. Liberia, about the size of Tennessee, with a population of over a million and situated on the southern side of West Africa, has a Constitution modeled on that of the United States.

Kennedy was aware of the tremendous political, economic, and social problems which the continent of Africa inevitably faced, and he intensified his efforts to establish between Africa and the United States cordial relationships based on mutual respect and understanding. He sent Assistant Secretary G. Mennen Williams to Africa, but when Williams in Nairobi endorsed the popular slogan, "Africa for the Africans," the President commented acidly: "I don't know who else Africa should be for."

He talked to Africans not as a partner of European colonial powers, but as an American endeavoring to see African problems the way Africans themselves saw them.

Colors: pink, black

At the United Nations General Assembly, during the special Commemorative Meeting held four days after Kennedy's assassination, Mr. Achkar Marof, Ambassador of Guinea, said, "As an African, I cannot fail to mention the prodigious activity, the clear-sighted determination, the unflagging courage of John F. Kennedy in the search for radical solutions to the racial problem, which he faithfully strove to settle equitably for the honor of his nation and the the dignity of man. Never did we feel closer to the American people and their brilliant President in the universal revolution for justice and freedom, served with such devotion by John F. Kennedy."

Sékou Touré, President of Guinea, had repeatedly invited Kennedy to visit his country. Unable to accept himself, the President sent his brother-in-law, Sargent Shriver, head of the Peace Corps, on two visits to Guinea.

The Republic of Guinea, a former French Overseas Territory, about the size of Oregon with a population of about three and a half million, is located in western Africa. It is rich in bauxite, iron, and diamonds. Its chief agricultural exports are bananas and pineapples.

Colors: pink, red, sepia   **44**

Kennedy was proud of the institution he created in his first hundred days—the Peace Corps.

The Peace Corps, as he envisioned it, was an organization of youthful volunteers who were willing to go to the underdeveloped regions of the world and live with the people in their villages, learn to speak their language, and work as teachers, nurses, carpenters, and technicians of all kinds. They received minimal compensation, but had the satisfaction of helping people who needed to be helped.

In some areas of the world these young Americans were known as "Kennedy's children," a term that describes fittingly how the President felt about them and how they felt about him. Older Americans may have thought him rather young to be President, but this did not appear to be the opinion of the young ones.

Burundi is mostly a cattle-raising and farming country. It is the home of the giant Watusi, the most graceful dancers of Africa. The Watusi were overlords and masters of the

Bahutu, a people of average height who made up the vast majority of the population. After independence in 1962, age-old resentments led to bloody uprisings. The Bahutu slew two Watusi premiers and severely wounded one.

The stamp shows Kennedy with Prime Minister Prince Louis Rwagasore who on October 13, 1961, was assassinated.

Colors: blue, aqua, sepia

When Burundi became independent in 1962, Mwami Mwambutsa IV was King. There was a premier and cabinet, an Assembly elected by universal suffrage and a Senate.

In 1964, King Mwambutsa came to the United States to see the New York World's Fair. On this occasion he visited Washington and stood in the Arlington cemetery next to the eternal light that burns on President Kennedy's grave. This scene is shown on the above stamp.

In July, 1966, the king's son, Prince Charles, a youth of nineteen, deposed him. He appointed a new cabinet, and on September 1 he was proclaimed Mwami King Ntare V.

About half of the population is Christian, mostly Roman Catholic. Many others believe in a supreme deity, Imana, the Principle of Good.

A Bantu language called Kirundi and French are the official languages. Swahili is also widely used.

The Charter has committed the United Nations to the independence of colonial peoples. On September 20, 1960, the General Assembly admitted no less than thirteen African nations. These nations, though independent, stood in need of assistance from the industrially developed nations to help them stand on their own feet economically as well as politically.

President Kennedy understood the plight of new nations and came to their aid. He said in his message to Congress, March 22, 1961: "We have a positive interest in helping less-developed nations provide decent living standards for their people and achieve sufficient strength, self-respect, and independence to become self-reliant members of the community of nations."

The Federation of Nigeria was one of the nations that became independent in 1960. Larger than Texas and Oklahoma combined, it is Africa's most populous country, comprising nearly two hundred and fifty tribal and linguistic groups. It is rich in natural resources, including palm oil, cotton, coal, cocoa, nuts, animal products, coal, iron, and tin.

Nigeria has chosen to remain within the British Commonwealth. Its capital is Lagos.

Colors: black, pink   **48**

  "John F. Kennedy, Friend of the African People." These are the words that Sierra Leone, "land of iron and diamonds," printed on its commemorative stamp.

  Kennedy made foreign aid a keystone of American policy. "A program of assistance to the underdeveloped nations must continue because the nation's interest and the cause of political freedom require it."

  The new nations, Kennedy said, "seek an end to injustice, tyranny, and exploitation. More than an end, they seek a beginning."

  Sierra Leone, an independent state within the British Commonwealth, is just a bit smaller than South Carolina and has a population of almost two and a half million. Freetown, the capital, was founded in 1788 by the British government as a home for destitute freed slaves.

  The name Sierra Leone, meaning Mountain of the Lion, was applied by an early Portuguese mariner because of the thunderstorms that roared about its coastal peaks.

Colors: yellow, cherry red, blue, light green

The Republic of Dahomey was among the thirteen African nations admitted to membership in the United Nations on September 20, 1960, forty-seven days before Kennedy was elected President. Dahomey, a country about the size of Pennsylvania, is in West Africa. It became fully independent August 1, 1960. A former French oversea territory, it chose to remain an autonomous state of the French Community of Nations, and retains close economic ties with France.

These young nations, poor and underdeveloped only a few years ago, are at present undergoing intensive economic development, which is transforming their way of life. President Kennedy was one of the initiators of these important changes. It was not simply a matter of idealism or generosity; he knew that the security and prosperity of these nations or of any nation will help in the long run to safeguard American and international security.

At the United Nations, Kennedy helped to launch an international "Decade of Development" to prevent the widening of the gap between the "haves" and the "have-nots" among nations.

Colors: black, dark green   **50**

This stamp has a strange history. When the Republic of Togo entered the United Nations in September, 1960, the group of delegates was headed by Prime Minister Sylvanus Olympio. On April 9, 1961, Mr. Olympio was elected President of his country. In March of 1962, he visited Washington and met John F. Kennedy.

Claude Bottiau, a French artist, was asked to prepare a stamp for Togoland in honor of this occasion and was given twenty-four hours. He used a reverse photograph of the Capitol for background and decorated the stamp with the portraits of the two presidents. It was the first stamp picturing Kennedy to appear while he was alive.

Ten months later, President Olympio was slain in Lomé, the capital of Togo, in front of the United States Embassy, toward which he was fleeing to find refuge. Nine months later, President Kennedy was slain in Dallas, Texas. After both presidents had suffered violent death, the stamp was turned into a commemorative stamp for both. The sheet today commands very high prices.

The Republic of Togo, in southern West Africa, is about twice the size of Vermont and has a population of over a million and a half. From 1946 to the year of its independence in 1960, it was administered by France as a trusteeship. Its constitution is modeled after that of the United States.

Colors: orange, green   51

PRESIDENT John F. KENNEDY
1917 - 1963

POSTE AERIENNE 100F

REPUBLIQUE
DU SENEGAL

"He was a valiant fighter in the noblest battle of humanity, the battle for peace between nations, for racial equality in his own country and in the world, for the emancipation of peoples, and for understanding between men." So spoke an eminent African leader, Benoit Bindizi, Vice-President of the United Nations General Assembly, at the special Commemorative Meeting, called on November 26, 1963.

Another African leader said of him: "In paying a profound tribute to the memory of this great man, we must reaffirm the desire of the African peoples and, without doubt, of all peoples throughout the world, to cooperate with the American people, to ensure the victory of freedom, justice, and peace on our planet."

"Since the close of World War II," President Kennedy had said in the very hall where this Commemorative Meeting was held, "a world-wide declaration of independence has transformed nearly one billion people and nine million square miles into forty-two free and independent states. . . .

"My country intends to be a participant, not merely an observer, in the peaceful, expeditious movement of nations from the status of colonies to the partnership of equals."

Senegal, in West Africa, is somewhat smaller than Nebraska, and has a population of three and a half million. In Dakar, its capital, the first World Festival of the Negro Arts was held in 1966, with the participation of the American band leader and composer, Duke Ellington, and poet Langston Hughes.

Colors: orange, sepia, dark green

SPACE TRAVEL

In 1957, the Soviet Union launched its space satellite, *Sputnik*, and was the first to put live animals into orbit. The United States started its own space program tardily. Kennedy feared that the Soviet successes would create an impression of unchallenged world leadership of the Russians in science and technology. In a special second State of the Union message in May, 1961, he made a dramatic pledge that the United States would land a man on the moon and return him safely to earth "before this decade is out."

New launching facilities were built in Houston, Texas, and Cape Canaveral, Florida (which is now called Cape Kennedy), and at several other sites.

These new steps in the space program were not taken without some grumbling on the part of taxpayers who complained about the high costs. Some political opponents called the program a "science fiction stunt."

Yet the nation was pleased when the first American, Commander Alan Shepard, was shot into space and returned to tell the tale.

Colors: black, light pink   **54**

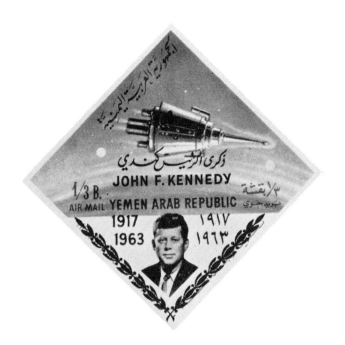

In September, 1962, at Rice University in Houston, Texas, Kennedy reaffirmed that the nation must "set sail on this new sea."

He said, "We choose to go to the moon in this decade, and do the other things, not because they are easy but because they are hard; because that goal will serve to organize and measure the best of our energies and skills; . . .

"Many years ago the great British explorer, George Mallory, who was to die on Mount Everest, was asked why he wanted to climb it. He said, 'Because it is there.'

"Well, space is there and . . . the moon and the planets are there, and new hopes for knowledge and peace are there."

The National Aeronautics and Space Administration (NASA) had ambitious plans: one-man orbits, two men in a spacecraft, an orbiting space laboratory, manned rocket around the moon, man landing on the moon, manned exploration of the planets.

Some of these plans have been realized since Kennedy revitalized the space program. Others are still to come.

Colors: black, blue, red, orange

The first real space-spectacular staged by the United States occurred in February, 1962, when Colonel John Glenn three times orbited the earth. Ten times the launching had been postponed because of technical difficulties, and during the flight itself dangers had threatened that might have caused Glenn to be burned alive. Immediately after Colonel Glenn's safe landing, the President talked to him over the telephone, and his excitement showed in his words of almost boyish gladness: "Listen, Colonel," he said, "we are really proud of you, I must say you did a wonderful job."

The stamp shows the President and Colonel Glenn at Cape Canaveral, standing before "Friendship 7" the capsule in which the colonel had made his trip. Behind the President stands Vice President Lyndon B. Johnson.

This stamp was issued by Ras al Khaima, one of the states of Trucial Oman on the Persian Gulf.

Colors: pink, ocher

At their Vienna meeting in 1961, Kennedy had suggested to Khrushchev a joint space exploration program, but the Soviet Chairman had shown little interest. He compared the United States' space progress with the evolution of insects, saying that the Soviet Union's space effort was already in the flying stage, while that of the United States was still at the jumping stage.

But after the flight of Colonel Glenn, he sent a telegram to the President, not only to congratulate him, but expressing interest in space cooperation. The President, in a letter to Khrushchev, repeated the proposals set forth in his first State of the Union message: joint weather satellite system, coordinated communications satellites, exchange of information in the field of space medicine, cooperative tracking arrangements and other common operations.

In his first speech before the United Nations Assembly in September, 1961, President Kennedy had said: "As we extend the rule of law on earth, so must we also extend it to man's new domain—outer space. . . . The cold reaches of the Universe must not become the new arena of an even colder war."

Colors: black, blue, red, orange   **57**

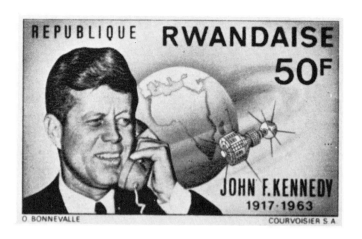

REPUBLIQUE RWANDAISE 50F
JOHN F. KENNEDY
1917-1963
O. BONNEVALLE
COURVOISIER S.A.

"To this end," said the President before the United Nations Assembly, "we shall urge proposals extending the United Nations Charter to the limits of man's exploration in the universe, reserving outer space for peaceful use, prohibiting weapons of mass destruction in space or on celestial bodies, and opening the mysteries and benefits of space to every nation. We shall further propose cooperative efforts in weather prediction and eventually weather control. We shall propose, finally, a global system of communications satellites linking the whole world by telegraph, telephone, radio, and television. The day need not be far away when such a system will televise the proceedings of this body to every corner of the world for the benefit of peace."

The stamp, issued by the Republic of Rwanda, depicts the President talking over the telephone to a faraway land via Telstar.

Rwanda, in East Central Africa, is about the size of Maryland and has a population of three million. The country was part of the former Belgian United Nations Trusteeship of Ruanda-Urundi. Coffee is the principal crop.

Colors: sepia, gray

58

Yemen territory is divided today into the Muta-wakelite Kingdom of Yemen and the Yemen Arab Republic.

Revolution broke out in September, 1962, and a revolutionary group declared the country a republic. But mountain tribesmen joined with royalist forces, and a civil war ensued, in which President Nasser supported the republican forces and King Faisal the royalist forces.

Both republicans and royalists issued stamps in honor of President Kennedy.

Colors: black, blue, orange

In both his inaugural and his first State of the Union message the President called for cooperation between East and West in space: "... to invoke the wonders of science instead of its terrors. Together let us explore the stars, ..."

In his speech before the United Nations, two months before his assassination, Kennedy came back to the idea of a joint Soviet-American expedition to the moon. The President asked the world organization why, since its members had forsworn claims to territorial rights in outer space, man's first flight to the moon should be a matter of national competition.

He did not succeed in eliminating the space race, but he did establish limited cooperation in such fields as space medicine, tracking, and rescue of stranded space travelers.

San Marino, the world's smallest republic, lies on the slope of Mount Titano in the Apennines, the heart of Italy. It is one-third the size of the District of Columbia and has a population of seventeen thousand. The army, which is maintained strictly for ceremonial use, has one hundred and eighty men. The principal industry is the printing of postage stamps and tourism. There is no unemployment in San Marino.

Colors: gray, red, blue, green

"Those who came before us made certain that this country rode the first waves of the industrial revolution, the first waves of modern invention and the first wave of nuclear power, and this generation does not intend to founder in the backwash of the coming age of space. We mean to be a part of it. We mean to lead it, for the eyes of the world now look into space, to the moon and to the planets beyond; and we have vowed that we shall not see it governed by a hostile flag of conquest, but by a banner of freedom and peace. We have vowed that we shall not see space filled with weapons of mass destruction, but with instruments of knowledge and understanding."

So spoke John Fitzgerald Kennedy at Rice University, Houston, Texas, September 12, 1962.

Colors: black, gold, light green   **61**

ALLIANCE FOR PROGRESS

On March 13, 1961, President Kennedy met in the East Room of the White House with the Latin American ambassadors stationed in Washington. It was the room in which, 139 years earlier, the United States had urged the recognition of the South American republics who were at that time fighting for their independence against Spain. Kennedy revealed to the ambassadors a ten-point program that became known as the Alliance for Progress, or *Alianza para el Progreso.*

The program was to demonstrate, in the President's words, "that man's unsatisfied aspirations for economic progress and social justice can best be achieved by free men working within a framework of democratic institutions. . . ." He called the *Alianza* "a vast cooperative effort, unparalleled in magnitude and nobility of purpose, to satisfy the basic needs of the American people for homes, work, land, health, and schools." He added in Spanish: *"Techo, trabajo y tierra, salud y escuela."* His Spanish had a Harvard accent, but it was received well by the South Americans.

Chile lies on the west coast of South America. It is slightly larger than Texas and has a population of over nine million. The arid deserts of northern Chile contain rich mineral wealth: nitrate, copper, iron, silver, gold, cobalt, and manganese. Seventy per cent of the world's iodine is a by-product of Chilean nitrate.

Color: blue

BARREIRO   J B GUREWITSCH

    The Alliance was formally organized in August, 1961, at a conference held at Punta del Este, Uruguay. In a message to that conference, where the delegates of twenty nations met, the President said, "We live in a hemisphere whose own revolution has given birth to the most powerful forces of the modern age—the search for the freedom and self-fulfillment of man. We meet to carry on that revolution to shape the future." And he pronounced his view of the future: "The full recognition of the rights of all the people to share fully in our progress. For there is no place in democratic life for institutions which benefit the few while denying the needs of the many."

    The conference drew up a charter signed by the twenty American republics in which they pledged, among other goals, "to accelerate economic and social development . . . to assure fair wages and satisfactory working conditions to all workers; to wipe out illiteracy; to press forward with programs of health and sanitation; to stimulate private enterprise."

The United States engaged to provide a major part of the twenty billion dollars Latin America would require over the next ten years.

Uruguay, somewhat larger than North Dakota, has a population of nearly three million. It is one of the most advanced republics in South America. Education, including college, is free.

Colors: black, green, gold

Each year the President visited Latin America, and on his arrival in Mexico City in June, 1962, he spoke of the Mexican Revolution, saying that the revolution of this hemisphere will be incomplete "until every child has a meal and every student has an opportunity to study, and everyone who wishes to work can find a job, and everyone who wishes a home can find one, and everyone who is old can have security."

Besides Mexico, the President visited Colombia, Venezuela, and Costa Rica. He was generally accompanied by his wife, Jacqueline, and they were received with wild enthusiasm.

The above stamp shows him with the Mexican President, Adolfo López Mateos, July 18, 1963, four months before his death.

Mexico, larger than the states of Alaska and Montana combined, with a population of over forty-four million, is the immediate neighbor of the United States to the south.

Mexico was the site of several advanced Indian cultures. The Mayas built immense stone pyramids and invented a calendar. The Toltecs were overcome by the Aztecs; and the Aztecs were overcome by Hernando Cortez, the Spanish conqueror, 1519–21. After three centuries of misrule, the people rose against Spain and made the country independent.

Mexico is rich in minerals and timber. The petroleum production is huge; agriculture, stock-raising, and fishing are important industries.

Colors: black, pink

The charter of Punta del Este, signed in Uruguay, was a call for a new revolution in Latin America, a democratic revolution; but most of the governments that signed were far from revolutionary. Some of their leaders no doubt signed it because they considered the promise and prospect of generous American aid worth a signature.

Lleras Camargo, the progressive and democratic President of Colombia, the country that issued the above stamp, explained, "In Latin America, perhaps more than anywhere else in the world, political leaders have the habit of carrying revolutionary statement beyond the point to which they are really prepared to go."

The progress of the *Alianza para el Progreso* has indeed been slow, though its task, as President Kennedy admitted, was "staggering in its dimensions." He contemplated this snail's pace progress with melancholy, and concerning it he once told his press conference that he felt "depressed"—a word he rarely used.

Colombia, situated in the extreme northwest of South

America, is about four times the size of Arizona, with a population of almost nineteen million. The country is rich in minerals and is a heavy producer of petroleum. Second only to Brazil in the export of coffee, Colombia ships approximately six and a half million bags, each weighing 132 pounds, a year.

Colors: blue, gray, sepia

The South Americans were not the only ones
to blame for the slow progress of the Alliance. American
business preferred to worry more about investments and
less about social reform, and many Latin Americans looked
upon these investments as a form of "Yanqui" imperialism.

From time to time violent revolution organized by military dictators further interrupted the work of the Alliance.
"We are opposed to military coups," Kennedy said, "because we think they are self-defeating . . . for the hemisphere."

To this day, opinions are divided as to whether the Alliance for Progress has been a success at all. It has not
realized its immediate goals, but the fact is that it has acted
as a stimulant, and a badly needed stimulant, to social
change in South America. Because of it teachers have been
trained, school children have been given textbooks and
extra food, tens of thousands of farm families have been
settled on their own land, and roads and houses have been
built. A tremendous return was given in terms of reinforced

solidarity in the hemisphere, for the American President was winning the affection of the Latin American people.

In Bogotá, Colombia, Kennedy was greeted by a wildly enthusiastic crowd. President Camargo said to Kennedy, "Do you know why these workers and *campesinos* are cheering you like that? It is because they believe you are on their side."

Argentina, the southernmost country of South America, is four times the size of Texas. Its chief industries are meat processing and flour milling. Its capital is Buenos Aires.

Colors: black, cherry red

President Kennedy was greatly disturbed by the attitude to the Alliance of that powerful 2 percent of the population in Latin America who own 50 percent of the wealth and control the press, newspapers, radio, and television, and who are especially influential with the armies. They considered the proposals made under the Alliance for social and political reforms a menace to stability and a threat to their privileges. Kennedy knew they would have to be persuaded. He advocated a peaceful democratic revolution, which would be achieved with the strengthening of everyone's fundamental freedoms.

Over and over again he told Latin Americans: "Those who make peaceful revolution impossible will make violent revolution inevitable." Such a revolution had already taken place in Fidel Castro's Cuba.

Had Castro been a communist when he took up arms against the dictator, Fulgencio Batista? Those who knew him in those days say that he was only a romantic left-wing nationalist. The communists of Cuba had called him a bourgeois, a rebel, adolescent and irresponsible. He himself admitted that when he tried to read Karl Marx's fundamental work *Das Kapital,* he couldn't get further than page 370.

Nicaragua, the country that issued this stamp, is the largest of the Central American states. It is essentially an agricultural country, but industrialization is increasing.

Colors: black, sepia

CUBA: THE BAY OF PIGS

In the beginning, Castro's revolution was subsidized by businessmen and landowners and supported by intellectuals. His avowed aim was to provide his land with free elections, a liberal constitution, civil liberties, and agrarian reforms.

But after he turned Communist and made a circus out of the execution of Batista's former supporters, many of those who had fought on his side in the Sierra Maestra turned against him and fled the country. Thousands of Cuban refugees settled in Florida and in Guatemala, with one idea—to return one day to their homeland and liberate their country from Castro.

In the spring of 1961, the planners of the Central Intelligence Agency warned the President that the time was now ripe for action, before the Russians began to build up Castro's army. They assured him that the invasion by the brigade of exiled Cubans could not fail.

On April 17, 1961, in the Zapata Swamp at the Bay of Pigs in Cuba, a force of some fourteen hundred anti-Castro exiles landed. In less than three days they were beaten, outnumbered by the forces of dictator Fidel Castro.

The involvement of the United States in this invasion was impossible to deny. The President spoke over television and publicly accepted sole responsibility for the disaster before the people and before the world.

The Organization of American States (OAS), to which the United States and all Latin American countries belong, at a conference held in January, 1962, declared that the present government of Cuba was incompatible with the inter-American system; and they therefore excluded Cuba from the OAS and called for collective defense against communist penetration of the hemisphere.

This stamp was issued by Brazil, an OAS member and the largest nation in South America both in population and in area. It is the world's greatest coffee grower and has vast mineral resources. The most important manufacturing industry is cotton weaving.

Color: gray

CORREOS DE EL SALVADOR
CENTRO AMERICA

6 Cts

JOHN FITZGERALD KENNEDY
22 NOVIEMBRE 1964

CUBAN MISSILE CRISIS

The Bay of Pigs invasion was a double disaster, because it really gave the Soviet Union an excuse to strengthen Castro's army. In late summer of 1962, secretly, rocket-launching pads were installed in Cuba, and by September nuclear weapons capable of striking at the United States were on their way. Premier Khrushchev gambled that once these missiles were in place, the United States would not risk a war for their removal. He was wrong.

The President called a meeting of the Executive Committee of the National Security Council, composed of civilians and military leaders, to decide what to do. Some suggested mild methods bringing diplomatic pressure to bear on the Soviet Union, including an appeal to the United Nations. Others wanted to take all the risks entailed by bombing the missile sites from the air.

The President decided to place a naval blockade which would prevent ships carrying military equipment from reaching the island, although on September 11 a Soviet statement had warned that any United States military action against Cuba would unleash nuclear war. In international law, a blockade enforced by arms is an act of war, so the President did not call it a blockade. He said it was a "quarantine," proving that roses by other names do smell sweeter, after all.

On Monday, October 22, 1962, President Kennedy, in a radio and television address told the American people of their imminent danger. In a calm, firm voice he said, "The purpose of these bases can be none other than to provide a nuclear strike capability against the Western Hemisphere." He said that the Soviet statement that only defensive weapons were being placed in Cuba was a "deliberate deception," and he warned the Soviets that the United States intended "to regard any nuclear missile launched from Cuba against any nation in the Western Hemisphere as an attack by the Soviet Union on the United States, requiring a full retaliatory response on the Soviet Union."

He told the nation and her allies the initial steps that were being taken: a quarantine on offensive military equipment on its way to Cuba, a request for an emergency meeting of the United Nations Security Council, and an appeal to Premier Khrushchev personally "to abandon this course of world domination and to join in an historic effort to end the perilous arms race. . . .

"Our goal," he said, "is not the victory of might, but the vindication of right; not peace at the expense of freedom, but both peace *and* freedom, here in this hemisphere, and, we hope, around the world."

While the President spoke, Cuban workmen were laboring night and day to complete the bases. Forty-five missiles were unpacked. Russian aircraft were assembled, and twenty-five Soviet merchant ships, loaded with military equipment, were steaming toward Cuba. The United States placed ninety ships, eight aircraft carriers, and sixty-eight aircraft squadrons in position to impose the quarantine.

Each Soviet ship was accompanied by a submarine, and each submarine was shadowed by an American destroyer.

Among the destroyers was the *Joseph P. Kennedy, Jr.*, named after the President's brother who had died in action.

The Navy's orders were to signal each approaching ship and stop it for inspection. Then, if no satisfactory response was forthcoming, to fire a shot across her bow. If still no satisfactory answer was received, a shot would be fired into her rudder, to cripple but not to sink.

In the meantime, in Florida and neighboring states, the largest United States invasion force since World War II was assembled.

The Soviet Union angrily insisted that the weapons being sent to Cuba were defensive. But at the United Nations, Ambassador Adlai Stevenson presented the evidence that they were offensive—aerial photographs, showing the missiles in Cuba. Valerian Zorin, the Soviet representative, promptly declared that they had been faked.

Mr. Stevenson said in defense of the quarantine, "Were we to do nothing until the knife was sharpened? Were we to stand idly by until it was at our throat? . . . Our job, Mr. Zorin, is to save the peace, and if you are ready to try, we are."

For the first time, the United States and Soviet Russia had faced each other with the possibility of nuclear war between them, war in which both nations could have been obliterated. In this fateful hour, the President asked his wife and children to return to the White House, to have them nearby.

Then came the break in the nuclear confrontation—not in the White House, or the Kremlin, or at the United Nations, but in the coffee shop of the Statler Hilton Hotel in Washington. There, a counselor of the Soviet Embassy approached a White House correspondent and sounded him out. If the Soviet Union, under United Nations inspection, were to remove the missiles, and Premier Khrushchev were to promise never to introduce such offensive weapons into Cuba again, did the correspondent think that the President of the United States would be willing to promise publicly not to invade Cuba?

The proposal was immediately relayed to the President. Soon the correspondent was able to report back to his Russian companion that the President saw real possibilities in the proposal. The Russian got so excited that he tossed five dollars on the table to pay the bill of thirty cents, and rushed away without waiting for the change.

Shortly afterward, the Soviet Union removed the missiles and the United States promised not to invade Cuba.

It is not without reason that El Salvador in Central America issued a stamp representing Kennedy with the olive branch, symbol of peace.

El Salvador, the smallest but most densely populated of the Central American republics, is about the size of Massachusetts. It is essentially an agricultural country. Its primary product is coffee, but it also grows corn, rice, beans, tobacco, and cotton.

Colors: black, ocher

UNITED NATIONS

In 1945, when the United Nations was born, young Jack Kennedy was in San Francisco as a journalist. As President he remained an ardent supporter of the UN, and in his inaugural address made a declaration of faith: "To that world assembly of sovereign states, the United Nations, our last best hope in an age where the instruments of war have far outpaced the instruments of peace, we renew our pledge of support—to prevent it from becoming merely a forum of invective—to strengthen its shield of the new and the weak—and to enlarge the area in which its writ may run."

He named Adlai Stevenson head of the permanent delegation.

Ecuador, which issued this stamp showing Kennedy before the United Nations Headquarters building, is somewhat larger than Arizona, with a population of over five million. It is situated on the northwestern coast of South America. The country is rich in undeveloped minerals—silver, copper, iron, and lead—and is the world's largest exporter of bananas.

Colors: black, red, blue

The President addressed the United Nations General Assembly twice. The first time was on September 25, 1961, and the second time on September 20, 1963, two months before his death. In both speeches he passed in review all the problems facing mankind: nuclear holocaust, disease, famine, arms race, space race, and the gap between developed nations and the new, developing ones.

"We prefer world law, in the age of self-determination," he said, "to world war, in the age of mass extermination. . . .

"Every man, woman, and child lives under a nuclear sword of Damocles, hanging by the slenderest of threads, capable of being cut at any moment by accident, miscalculation, or madness. The weapons of war must be abolished before they abolish us."

And he said: "It is therefore our intention to challenge the Soviet Union not to an arms race, but to peace race: to advance with us step by step, stage by stage, until general and complete disarmament has actually been achieved."

He supported the notion of a United Nations police force. "The United States recommends that all member nations earmark special peace-keeping units in their armed forces, to be on call to the United Nations, to be especially trained and quickly available, and with advance provision for financial and logistic support."

Secretary General Dag Hammarskjöld also wanted to work out a method of having standby peacekeeping forces available, but this has not yet come to pass.

Colors: black, ocher, blue

Kennedy pledged and gave full support to the new nations. It was he who proposed that the 1960's should be officially designated the "United Nations Development Decade."

"My nation was once a colony, and we know what colonialism means: the exploitation and subjugation of the weak by the powerful, of the many by the few, of the governed who have given no consent to be governed, whatever their continent, their class, or their color."

Qatar is an independent Arab sheikdom, situated on a peninsula on Arabia's northeast coast, with a population of almost sixty thousand. The country is rich in oil. Though the International Cooperation year was in 1965, two years after the President's death, Qatar recognized that it was in the spirit of his thinking, and they chose to honor him with the above stamp.

Colors: aqua, sepia, pink   **84**

JOHN F. KENNEDY 1917·1963

60ᶠ

COURAGE
PATRIOTISME
SINCERITE

RÉPUBLIQUE
DÉMOCRATIQUE du CONGO

CONGO TROUBLES

On June 30, 1960, the Belgian Congo became independent. No country was less prepared. Within days the Congolese army mutinied and ran rampant over the land. When the Belgians flew paratroopers into the country to restore order, the country, in panic, fell apart. Some provinces declared their independence.

President Kasavubu and Premier Lumumba turned to the United Nations for assistance. Secretary General Dag Hammarskjöld hastily set up an emergency force known as ONUC *(Operation des Nationes Unies au Congo)*. But Mr. Lumumba turned also to the Soviet Union, and Khrushchev, seeing a chance for a foothold in Africa, sent him one hundred military trucks, twenty-nine airplanes, and two hundred technicians. The situation was at its blackest when Lumumba was kidnapped and murdered, and Dag Hammarskjöld, who had tried his best to keep the Congo together, was killed in an air crash which some people believe was also deliberately caused.

85

ONUC was not equipped to prevent the full scale civil war which threatened to break out in the fall of 1961.

Then, at the request of the new Secretary General, U Thant, Kennedy sent American planes, trucks, and armored vehicles to the Congo. By this timely action the country's territorial integrity was restored.

The failure to keep order in the Congo was laid at the door of the United Nations, and the world organization was at the brink of bankruptcy. It was Kennedy who helped to launch a "Peace Loan" that helped the UN to her feet again.

The inscription on the stamps is in French. It reads: courage, patriotism, sincerity.

Until June, 1960, the Congo was a colony of Belgium. A country the size of Texas and Alaska combined, it is situated in equatorial Africa, where the wildlife includes most of the species Africa is famous for: elephant, lion, gorilla, hippopotamus, python. The Congo is the world's largest producer of cobalt and industrial diamonds.

Colors: black, sepia

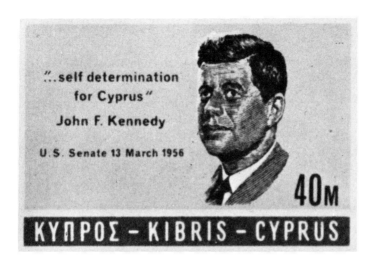

"...self determination for Cyprus"
John F. Kennedy
U.S. Senate 13 March 1956

40M

ΚΥΠΡΟΣ - ΚΙΒRΙS - CYPRUS

OTHER TROUBLE SPOTS

The Congo was not the only trouble spot in the world. There was a growing crisis in Cyprus, where the Greek and Turkish population were in constant clash.

In Laos, the local communists were pressing upon the democratic government. A conference was called in Geneva, and with the participation of Red China and North Vietnam, an agreement was worked out which was by no means a perfect agreement, but it was better than war. Still unrest had prevailed in this area for some time, and in neighboring Vietnam it culminated in war. Kennedy inherited these troubles from the previous administration. As in Laos, his desire was to halt the communist-sponsored guerrilla war and permit the local population to choose its own form of government. By 1961, Vietcong guerrillas were gradually bleeding South Vietnam to death. American instructors, accompanying Vietnamese forces, were being killed.

Kennedy ordered the Defense Department to be prepared

for the introduction of combat troops, should they prove to be necessary. He increased the number of military missions—two thousand men at the end of 1961, fifteen thousand at the end of 1963—and he sent six hundred of the "Green Berets," which he founded as a special force, to train South Vietnamese in guerrilla tactics.

Cyprus, with a population of over six hundred thousand, is the third largest island in the Mediterranean Sea. Four fifths of the inhabitants are Greek Orthodox Christians; the rest are Turkish Moslems; and they could not get along with each other. The problem for the United States was that two NATO allies, Greece and Turkey, were involved in the dispute. Finally the United Nations sent in a police force which succeeded in keeping the belligerents apart.

Color: green

KENNEDY THE ORATOR

Kennedy's speeches were exceptionally rousing and inspiring. They were excellent rhetoric. After his special assistant, Sorensen, had studied Lincoln's Gettysburg address, he was able to report to his chief that Lincoln had never used a two- or three-syllable word where a one-syllable word would do, and had never used two or three words where one would do.

When the President needed to inform the American people of the Cuban missile crisis, Sorensen studied the speeches of Woodrow Wilson and Franklin D. Roosevelt when they had declared World War I and World War II. The President's speech before the United Nations in 1961 was written on the plane as he was traveling from Hyannis Port to New York. The presidential compartment was so full of people and so noisy that the President and Sorensen had sat on the floor in the corridor where they worked on the speech.

He liked to use sentences in counterpoint: "Let us never

negotiate out of fear. But let us never fear to negotiate." He also preferred sentences and ideas that ended with a snap, as when he said before the Canadian Parliament: "Geography has made us neighbors; history made us friends; economics made us allies. Those whom nature has so joined together, let no man put asunder."

He also liked to hammer at his points, as in "We shall pay any price, bear any burden, meet any hardship, support any friend, oppose any foe to assure the survival and success of liberty."

In such sentences there was a progressive rhythm in the words as well as in the thought. He never memorized a speech, and sometimes he improvised. He wanted short speeches, "I don't want people to think I'm a windbag," he said.

Colors: black, red, blue,
apple green

JFK

The President went to his office quarters at eight in the morning. As he sat down to his breakfast tray, Caroline and John would rush in, greet their father, and turn on the television set to watch animated cartoons. Amid the squeak of Mighty Mouse and the growls of Yogi Bear, the President would read the morning papers and incoming cables from all over the world.

Then the telephone went into action, for the President liked to keep in personal touch with every detail of business of state.

He lunched alone or with Jacqueline, and after lunch he took a nap—a real nap, in pajamas and under covers. He fell asleep like a log, but forty-five minutes later he would awaken promptly, as if equipped with a built-in alarm clock.

He took at least three swims a day in the heated White House pool, to relieve his aching back.

He enjoyed living in the White House, unlike Thomas

Jefferson who had called it "a splendid misery," or Truman, for whom it was the "finest prison in the country." He used to say, with tongue in cheek, "I have a nice home, the office is close by, and the pay is good."

He had an appetite for work; at meetings he could "out-listen" everybody, but if it went on too long, his fingers would begin to drum on the table or he would tap his teeth or doodle violently.

He could lose his temper, but his anger did not last.

As a singer he could carry a tune, and that was about all. Once in Dorchester, Massachusetts, too tired to deliver a campaign speech, he seized the arms of his brothers Robert and Teddy and presented "The Three Kennedy Brothers" singing "Heart of My Heart." But he never played the clown on campaign tours, never put on firemen's helmets, ten-gallon hats, or the headgear of an Indian chief as many campaigning politicians do. He could be boyish, but he took his work seriously.

In his office he seldom worked in shirtsleeves, though sometimes he would pull out the tail of his shirt to clean his glasses. He never wore a ring or any jewelry, except the famous PT boat tie clip.

His handwriting was a disgrace.

Malta, which issued this stamp, lies in the Mediterranean Sea. It is an island about twice the size of the District of Columbia and with a population of over three hundred thousand. Exports include potatoes, flowers, seeds, wine, paints, and rubber and plastic goods.

Colors: black, gray, gold

He poked fun at the mighty, including himself. He had no passion for cards, dice, or any gambling games, although he liked to bet on his golf games and consistently won bets on the World Series.

While impeccably correct on the platform or in society, his language and humor in private could be coarse, a characteristic he shared with Abraham Lincoln.

He did not smoke cigarettes; sometimes after a meal or during a conference, he would smoke a thin cigar. He drank quantities of milk and sometimes a bottle of beer. His father used to give a thousand dollars to all the Kennedy boys who did not smoke or drink before the age of twenty.

He did not fish or hunt, and he shuddered when Caroline showed him a dead bird she intended to bury.

His memory was excellent. He had the gift of sensing the kernel of an issue in seconds. He was a practical man and an idealist as well. He wrote in the book of his aide, Sorensen, "Every President must endure the gap between what he would like and what is possible."

"He was an idealist," said his wife, "without illusions."

Colors: blue, ocher

He had a gentle sense of irony that was directed against himself as well as against others. He kept a large humor folder, containing anecdotes which he used in his campaign speeches. One joke of his that backfired was told to a Washington audience when he was a young Senator. "The cab driver did such a good job rushing me to this luncheon," he said, "that I was going to give him a big tip and tell him to vote Democratic. Then I remembered the advice of Senator Green, so I gave him no tip and told him to vote Republican." The next day, he got an avalanche of protesting letters from cab drivers and their wives.

The first day in office in the White House, he told his assistant, "Telephone so and so, and say that the Senator wishes this and that . . ." Then he caught himself short with a laugh, remembering that he was not Senator, but President. Making a new start, he paraphrased Truman's criticism of him at the convention, asking, "Do you think the country is ready for us yet?"

In Ireland he was presented with a specially designed

O'Kennedy coat of arms. His wife had the device made into a seal ring for him. But since he did not like rings, he kept it on his desk. One day he told his wife with a smile, "I used my Irish seal on a letter today—to the Queen of England."

The White House played its part in the cultural life of the country. Great artists were asked to perform, and scientists were invited there. Once, at a dinner honoring American Nobel Prize winners, the President surveyed them and said, "This is the most extraordinary collection of talent . . . that has ever been gathered together at the White House— with the possible exception of when Thomas Jefferson dined alone."

The Dominican Republic occupies the eastern two-thirds of the Hispaniola Island, situated between Cuba and Puerto Rico. Its capital city, Santo Domingo, founded in 1496, is the oldest continuous European settlement in the hemisphere. The land is very fertile, and agriculture and stock raising are the principal activities.

Colors: orange, sepia

CORREOS DEL ECUADOR AEREO S/. 4.00

SIR WINSTON CHURCHILL
NOV. 3 1874 – ENE. 24 1965

JOHN F. KENNEDY
MAYO 29 1917-NOV. 22 1963

DE LA RUE DE COLOMBIA

During his tenure of office, Kennedy visited eleven countries and sat together with the chiefs of state. He received more than fifty presidents, prime ministers, and royal persons in the White House. He considered Charles de Gaulle "a wise counselor for the future." He did not share the view some people have that De Gaulle was merely a nineteenth-century romantic.

He respected the accomplishments of Konrad Adenauer, Chancellor of West Germany, but said, "I sense I am talking not to a different generation, but to a different era, a different world."

He was particularly fond of the Mayor of West Berlin, Willy Brandt, later co-chancellor of West Germany.

Like most young intellectuals of his generation, the President had a particular admiration for Jawaharlal Nehru of India; yet at the time they met he found Nehru tired and less interesting and stimulating than he had thought he would be.

Kennedy got along wonderfully well with Khrushchev,

in spite of their differences in age and culture. Both men were fully alive to the potential menace of the bomb. An intensive personal correspondence developed between the two, and a "hot line" was installed between the Kremlin and the White House. When Kennedy addressed American University in Washington, Khrushchev called it the best speech an American President had ever made.

Although the stamp on this page shows Kennedy in the company of Churchill, he really had little to do with that English Prime Minister, though much with his successor Harold Macmillan. Once he quoted Churchill who said, "It is better to jaw, jaw, than war, war," to which Kennedy added, "and we shall continue to jaw, jaw."

Colors: black, blue, sepia

STRATEGY OF PEACE

"The basic problems facing the world today are not susceptible to a military solution," said Kennedy in his message to Congress, March 21, 1961.

He was a man of peace, aware that in the atomic age the more nations arm, the more insecure they become. He told the United Nations that the task of peace lay with the leaders of every nation large and small, for the great powers were not the only ones prone to conflict or ambition. "Even little wars are dangerous in a nuclear world," he said. "The long labor of peace is an undertaking for every nation, and in this effort none of us can remain unaligned. To this goal, none can be uncommitted. . . .

"But I would say to the leaders of the Soviet Union, and to their people, that if either of our countries is to be fully secure, we need a much better weapon than the H-bomb, a weapon better than ballistic missiles or nuclear submarines, and that better weapon is peaceful cooperation."

By the summer of 1963, a draft treaty on this issue was drawn up, and the President sent his favorite troubleshooter, Averell Harriman, to Moscow at the head of a delegation to negotiate the treaty. They met Khrushchev, and on July 25 the treaty that banned nuclear testing in the atmosphere and under water was concluded and initialed.

Kennedy faced harsh criticism in Washington for this. He was accused of having made "a secret treaty with Khrushchev." The treaty was called a "greater risk to the national security than an arms race," and "for more tragic than no agreement at all."

The President took his case to the American people in a television address: "Yesterday a shaft of light cut into the darkness.... This treaty is not the millennium.... But it is an important first step—a step toward peace, a step toward reason, a step away from war.... This treaty is for all of us. It is particularly for our children and our grandchildren, and they have no lobby here in Washington....

"According to the ancient Chinese proverb, 'A journey of a thousand miles must begin with a single step.'... Let us take the first step."

The Senate ratified the treaty. France and Red China were invited to join, but both refused.

The independent sheikdom of Qatar issued this stamp showing President Kennedy with the Statue of Liberty, which is known throughout the world as the symbol of the democratic ideal.

Colors: black, blue, orange, green

In 1961, in his State of the Union address, the President said, "On the Presidential coat of arms, the American eagle holds in his right talon the olive branch, while in his left he holds a bundle of arrows. We intend to give equal attention to both."

While he tendered the olive branch to the world, in three years, at the cost of some seventeen billion dollars, he built up the most powerful military force in human history. Nevertheless, in a report to the people on July 25, 1961, he said, "While we are ready to defend our interests, we we shall also be ready to search for peace." He knew that in an armed conflict, neither the Soviet Union nor the United States could "win" a nuclear war. A "surprise" missile attack can trigger massive retaliation, even before those missiles reach their target. It did not matter who fired first or was annihilated last. "So we have to proceed with . . . care in an age when the human race can obliterate itself."

Before American University in Washington, D. C., June 10, 1963, talking of world peace, he said, "What kind of peace do I mean? What kind of peace do we seek? Not a *Pax*

Americana enforced on the world by American weapons of war. Not the peace of the grave or the security of the slave. I am talking about genuine peace, the kind of peace that makes life on earth worth living . . . not merely peace for Americans, but peace for all men and women; not merely peace in our own time, but peace for all time."

On Friday, November 22, 1963, in Dallas, Texas, an assassin's bullet put an end to his life.

Dubai, which issued this memorial stamp, is one of the seven sheikdoms of Trucial Oman on the Persian Gulf. Dubai is the main port.

Colors: light ocher, sepia

THE ASSASSINATION

When the shot was fired that Friday in Dallas, Jacqueline Kennedy, who was sitting in the car next to the President, cried out loud: "Oh, no, no . . . Oh my God, they have shot my husband!"

The wounded President was hurried to the Parkland Memorial Hospital, four miles away. On his arrival, he still had a heartbeat, but no beat of pulse was detectable. At one o'clock he was pronounced dead.

Jacqueline Kennedy was with him when they put his body in the casket. There she said farewell with a kiss and slipped the wedding ring from her own finger onto his.

Vice President Johnson left the Parkland Hospital and proceeded to the presidential plane that now carried Kennedy's body back to Washington, D. C. Shortly after, Mrs. Kennedy boarded the plane. In the central compartment of the plane, Lyndon B. Johnson was sworn in as the thirty-sixth President of the United States. In Washington, John F. Kennedy's body was taken to the National Naval Medical Center at Bethesda, Maryland, where it was prepared for the funeral.

Along with the President's brother, Rober F. Kennedy, Mrs. Kennedy remained at the Medical Center until her husband's body was returned to the White House to lie in state in the East Room. It was morning before she left his side for the painful duty of trying to find words to tell her children what had happened.

On Sunday morning, Jacqueline Kennedy, dressed in black and with a black lace mantilla, together with her children followed the flag-draped casket in a cortege to the rotunda of the Capitol, where the body was to lie in state; and the dignitaries of the land and 250,000 people came to pay their last tribute to the dead President.

In a moment of silent sorrow, Caroline and her mother walked to the bier and knelt beside it.

This memorial stamp was issued by Umm al Qiwain, one of the seven semi-independent sheikdoms of Trucial Oman on the Persian Gulf.

Colors: black, gold, light green

At St. Matthew's Cathedral, Cardinal Cushing, who had married them and christened their children and buried their infant son Patrick, met the bereaved family outside and bent to caress Caroline and John Junior before they entered the church behind the Cross. The Cardinal said a low requiem mass.

In regal dignity, heavily veiled, Jacqueline Kennedy stood between her brothers-in-law, Senator Edward Kennedy and Attorney General Robert Kennedy, with her children. After the mass was over the children were taken back to the White House without their mother.

It was Jacqueline Kennedy who had designated the site of the President's grave in Arlington Cemetery, on a little hill in front of the Custis-Lee Mansion, with the Lincoln Memorial visible in the distance. In a way, John F. Kennedy himself had chosen it. One warm March day, he had slipped out to Arlington with a friend. Looking at the magnificent view of Washington to be seen from this spot, he had said, "I could stay here forever."

Colors: black, gold, light pink   **104**

ARLINGTON CEMETERY

It took an hour to drive to Arlington National Cemetery. Three pairs of matched gray horses drew the caisson, and following the military custom, the right row of horses was saddled but riderless.

By age-old tradition, a riderless horse followed the casket carrying empty boots reversed in the stirrups, a sign that the warrior would not mount again. Muffled drums beat out the cadence of the march, and, above, fifty jet fighters roared —one dipping its wings in a special salute.

Behind the coffin rode the great of the world. Among them were President Charles de Gaulle of France, Chancellor Ludwig Erhard of Germany, Prime Minister Sir Alec Douglas-Home of Britain, First Deputy Premier Anastas Mikoyan of the Soviet Union, Prince Philip of Britain, Irish President Eamon de Valera, Philippine President Macapagal, Queen Frederika of Greece.

Colors: black, gold, light green   **105**

Not only kings, queens, presidents, and prime ministers paid tribute to the departed President; plain people all over the world were touched to the core. In New Delhi, people cried in the streets. In Poland, the church bells tolled for fifteen minutes, and university students gathered in masses to mourn him. In Latin America, his pictures were torn from the newspapers and hung on the walls of workers' shacks. In Kampala, Ugandans came to sit silently on the lawn of the American Embassy for hours on end, waiting for nothing. In N'zerekore, a group of natives presented a sum of money to an American pastor to buy a rush mat in which to bury the President, according to their custom. In the Sudan, an old Bishmarine tribesman told an American that it was terrible Kennedy's son was so young; it would be a long time before he could become a true leader.

An African magazine for intellectuals, *Transition*, wrote: "In this way was murdered the first real chance in this century for an intelligent and new leadership to the world. . . . More than any other person he achieved the intellectual's ideal of a man of action. His death leaves us unprepared and in darkness."

Colors: black, gold, light aqua   **106**

This stamp from Umm al Qiwain depicts two former Presidents, Dwight D. Eisenhower and Harry S. Truman, paying their last tribute to their successor. With them is Truman's daughter, Margaret.

During the campaign, Eisenhower had said harsh words about Nixon's opponent, but when Kennedy was elected, he sent a warm congratulatory message. Early in December, before Kennedy took office, they had had their first formal meeting and talked for seventy-five minutes. They walked arm in arm into the Cabinet Room, and later Eisenhower said that he was "overwhelmed by Senator Kennedy, his understanding of the world problems, the depth of his questions, his grasp of the issues, and the keenness of his mind."

Yet they were very different men, in religion, political philosophy, and in background: one from the Middle West, a "grass roots" American, educated at the straitlaced Military Academy; the other a New Englander, with an international background and an education at Harvard.

During the campaign, Truman had objected to Kennedy's youth. But after Kennedy was nominated he paid Truman a visit in Independence, soliciting his support, and Truman assured him of it. When the new President took up residence in the White House, Truman, who had not set foot in the presidential mansion since he had quitted it in 1952, was his first visitor.

Now the old had come to bury the young. They might have remembered the words of Solomon: "Having fulfilled his course in a short time, he fulfilled long years."

Colors: black, green, light pink

In 1961, Charles de Gaulle had toasted Kennedy's "intelligence and courage." And as Kennedy departed from Paris, De Gaulle had said, "I have more confidence in your country now." In spite of all their differences over the European Common Market, NATO, and nuclear testing, the two men continued to admire each other, and Kennedy maintained that "if trouble comes, General de Gaulle, as he has in the past, will definitely meet his responsibilities."

In September, 1962, De Gaulle sent word that he liked Kennedy, had enjoyed their last meeting, and would like to see him again. But their next meeting took place in Arlington.

Next to De Gaulle stood the King of Kings, the Lion of Judah, Haile Selassie, the Negus of Ethiopia. In 1936, when Mussolini had attacked Ethiopia, his country had been betrayed by the League of Nations. Now the Emperor stood at the grave of the man who in the United Nations had upheld the right to independence of all African nations.

Behind the Emperor of Ethiopia, head bowed, stood Ludwig Erhard, Chancellor of West Germany. He had come to bury a friend who had said in West Berlin: *"Ich bin ein Berliner"*—I am a Berliner; a friend who had been ready to go to war for the independence of the city.

It was a clear, cold day in the Arlington Cemetery.

Colors: black, gold, light green

At the grave there were final prayers, and the crack of a rifle volley bade farewell to the departed chief. The honor guard removed the flag that had covered John F. Kennedy's coffin for three days, smartly folding it into a triangle and handing it to his wife. She took it in both hands and put it under her left arm.

Shortly afterward, she stepped forward to light the eternal flame. It had been her own suggestion to have "something living" at the grave. As she turned away there were tears on her face behind the veil.

Late on Monday afternoon, Jacqueline Kennedy became a private person. That night she moved out of the White House and went back to the cemetery to visit once more her husband's grave, and to leave on it a sprig of lilies of the valley.

The next evening when the crowd had gone, she took Caroline to see her father's grave. She visited the spot again to witness the reburial in Arlington of her two lost children: One baby had been stillborn and another had died after two days. Both were laid near their father.

Colors: black, gold, light aqua

DADDY

"He's not the President, he's my daddy," Caroline had once said. These simple words summed up part of the essence of the tragedy. Caroline had lost her daddy, and the country had lost a President. When such a thing happens, the country can elect a new President, but the family's loss is irreparable. And yet for a time this did not seem to be the case. The entire country mourned with the family, sharing its grief, longing to extend comfort.

On the Sunday night that her husband's body lay in state, Mrs. Kennedy paid an impromptu visit to the Capitol; as she left the building a woman came out of the darkness and silently hugged her.

On that same Sunday little John Junior, in the Speaker's office, had been given a flag to play with to keep him quiet. He had asked for another, saying, "For my daddy."

Then when he stood before the coffin, he had lifted his small hand in a salute, just as he had seen the soldiers do.

Colors: red, blue, pink, sepia

112

REPUBLICA DE HONDURAS
1809   AEREO   1959
CONMEMORATIVA DEL
CL ANIVERSARIO DEL
NACIMIENTO DE LINCOLN

OFICIAL

50   ORACIÓN DE GETTYSBURG   50
CINCUENTA CENTAVOS DE LEMPIRA

LINCOLN AND KENNEDY

1963 was the centenary of Lincoln's Emancipation Proclamation. The parallel of Lincoln's and Kennedy's
life and death was so obvious that countries like Honduras
and Togo, that had issued Lincoln memorial stamps, simply
overprinted them, "To the memory of John F. Kennedy."
When Negro leader Rev. Martin Luther King Jr. visited
the White House and the President and Mrs. Kennedy had
shown him the room where Lincoln had signed the Emancipation Proclamation, King said, "Mr. President, I'd like
you to come back in this room one day and sit down at the
desk and sign the Second Emancipation Proclamation."
King was gratified when the President sent troops to the
University of Mississippi to put down the bloody riot and
protect James Meredith, who had tried to enroll as a
student.
"I like the way he talked about what we are getting,"
recollected King. "It wasn't something that he was getting
for the Negroes. You knew you had an ally."
On August 28, 1963, King marched at the head of a

throng of 230,000 people, brought them to Washington, and moved them to tears with his visionary oration, "I have a dream." That night he went to the White House.

Kennedy reached out and took his hand. "I have a dream," the President said.

This memorial stamp was issued by Honduras, a republic about the size of Pennsylvania, in Central America. The mountainous terrain of the country has hindered development. Mineral resources are abundant but undeveloped, and the chief export is bananas.

Colors: red, blue, cherry red

The stamp of Togo shows a broken chain and the flame of the eternal light, coming from the United States and illuminating Africa. It celebrates Lincoln and the centenary of the Emancipation, but the overprint is in memory of Kennedy.

The tragic fate of the two men haunted Jacqueline Kennedy on the night her husband died. She had sent somebody to an upstairs library in the White House to find a certain book about Lincoln which contained photographs and drawings of the ceremonies surrounding the lying-in-state and funeral. She remembered exactly where the book was, and she wanted everything to correspond as nearly as possible to what had been done for Lincoln. She even specified that the catafalque upon which the coffin would rest in the East Room should duplicate that of Lincoln.

And so it did.

Colors: green, ocher, black, gray

On September 22, when the crowd had gathered at the Lincoln Memorial to celebrate the first century of Emancipation, the President had said, "I believe that Abraham Lincoln emancipated the slaves, but that in this century since, our Negro citizens have emancipated themselves. . . . But the task is not finished.

"Like the proclamation we celebrate," he said, "this observance must be regarded not as an end, but as a beginning."

Martin Luther King Jr. said, "There were in fact two John Kennedys. One presided in the first two years under pressure of the uncertainty caused by a razor-thin victory. In 1963, a new Kennedy had emerged. . . . He was, at his death, undergoing a transformation from a hesitant leader with unsure goals to a strong figure with deeply appealing objectives."

The parallel with Lincoln was remarked by the delegate of El Salvador at the Commemorative Meeting of the General Assembly at the United Nations: "By his death, President Kennedy achieved immortality, and like Abraham Lincoln, he will be the finest model that history will present to coming generations."

Colors: red, blue, sepia

116

MAN OF PEACE

The Maldive Islands are a group of several atolls in the Indian Ocean, with a population of close to a hundred thousand. Their government chose to celebrate Kennedy as a man of peace.

In his commencement address at American University in 1963, the President had talked of his strategy for peace.

"I speak of peace because of the new face of war. Total war makes no sense . . . in an age when a single nuclear weapon contains almost ten times the explosive force delivered by all the Allied air forces in the Second World War. It makes no sense in an age when the deadly poisons produced by a nuclear exchange would be carried by the wind and water and soil and seed to the far corners of the globe and to generations yet unborn. . . .

"I realize that the pursuit of peace is not as dramatic as the pursuit of war, and frequently the words of the pursuer fall on deaf ears. But we have no more urgent task. . . .

"Our problems are man-made; therefore they can be solved by man. And man can be as big as he wants."

Whatever man builds is built on the sands of time, but ideas are eternal. President Kennedy is dead, but he continues to lead through the ideas he implanted in all of us. He was one of those remarkable men whose thoughts are like bridges into the future. Certainly it is a bridge that disappears into the distance but as he said, "A journey of a thousand miles begins with a step."

Colors: sepia, pink

This United States stamp shows the President with the eternal light that marks his grave at Arlington Cemetery. The first sheet was given to Mrs. Rose Kennedy, mother of the late President, by Postmaster General John A. Gronouski. The message on the border was taken from John Kennedy's inaugural address, in which he said, "In the long history of the world, only a few generations have been granted the role of defending freedom in its hour of maximum danger. I do not shrink from this responsibility —I welcome it. I do not believe that any of us would exchange places with any other people or any other generation. The energy, the faith, the devotion which we bring to this endeavor will light our country and all who serve it—and the glow from that fire can truly light the world."

Color: blue-gray   **119**

BIBLIOGRAPHY

Goldman, Alex J., *The Quotable Kennedy,* New York, Citadel Press, 1965.

Homage to a Friend, A Memorial Tribute by the United Nations, New York, U.S. Committee for the United Nations in cooperation with the U.N. Office of Public Information, 1964.

JFK Memorial Issue, Look Magazine, Vol. 28 (November 17, 1964), pp. 33–46.

The John F. Kennedy Memorial Edition, New York, *Life* Magazine.

Lieberson, Goddard, and Meyers, J. (eds.), *John Fitzgerald Kennedy as We Remember Him,* New York, Atheneum, 1965.

Miller, L., "The Delightful World of Caroline Kennedy," *Redbook,* Vol. 117 (June, 1961), pp. 34–74.

The New York Times Magazine, November 6, 1960.

Official Records of the United Nations, September 25, 1961; September 20, 1963.

Schlesinger, Arthur M., Jr., *A Thousand Days: John F. Kennedy in the White House,* Boston, Houghton Mifflin Co., 1965.

Sorensen, Theodore C., *Kennedy,* New York, Harper & Row, Publishers, 1965.

Time Magazine, July 11, 1960; November 7, 1960; November 16, 1960; January 20, 1961.

INDEX